People Live in the Desert

Belle Perez

Contents

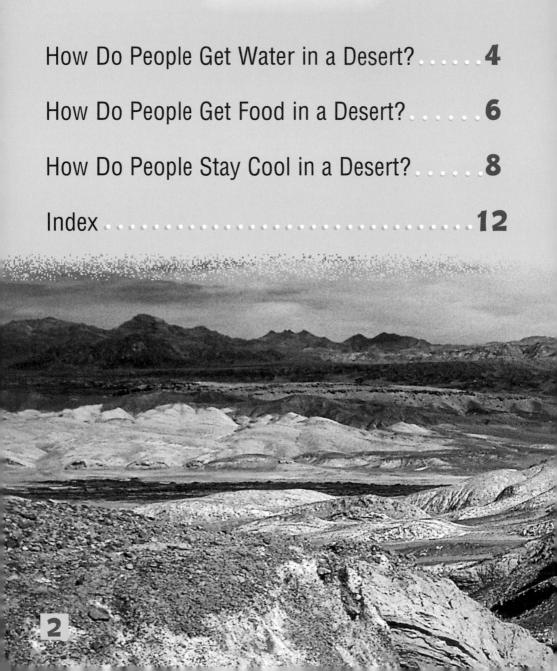

A desert is a hot, dry place.

How do people live in a desert?

How Do People Get Water in a Desert?

People dig wells.

They dig holes to get water from under the ground.

That's one way people get water in the desert.

People build pipelines.

The pipelines bring water from far away.

That's another way people get water in the desert.

How Do People Get Food in a Desert?

People grow food.

They bring in water to grow crops.

That's one way people get food in the desert.

People use trucks to bring in food.

The trucks bring food from far away.

That's another way people get food in the desert.

How Do People Stay Cool in a Desert?

People build houses from dried mud.

The thick mud walls keep out the heat.

That's one way people stay cool in the desert.

8

People build houses with air-conditioners.

The air-conditioners cool the air inside.

That's another way people stay cool in the desert.

People find ways to live in a desert.
They find ways to get water,
to get food, and to stay cool.

Index